THOMAS HARDY

His Life and Landscape

Desmond Hawkins

The National Trust

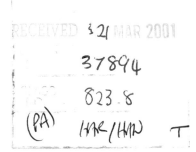

THOMAS HARDY, now internationally famous as a novelist and a poet, was born near Dorchester in a cottage on the edge of what he named 'Egdon' Heath on 4 June 1840. In the succeeding 150 years many of the landscapes and buildings that feature in his stories and poems have attracted visitors because of those associations: that they are able to do so is often due to the care and forethought of the National Trust, which carries a great responsibility for our West Country heritage, in literature no less than in architecture and the conservation of nature.

Hardy's father was a jobbing builder in a small way of business. His mother grew up in poverty and was placed in domestic service at an early age. They had four children, of whom Thomas was the eldest; all four died childless. Their home had been built by the author's great-grandfather, John Hardy, for his newly married son, Thomas Hardy the First. A map of part of the Kingston Maurward estate in the parish of Stinsford in 1800 shows a new development in the hamlet of

Springtime in Thorncombe wood behind Hardy's Cottage.

The garden of the cottage at Higher Bockhampton, near Dorchester, where Thomas Hardy was born in 1840. It was bought by the National Trust in 1948 and is stocked with the old varieties of English flowers described by Hardy in his early poem, 'Domicilium':

Red roses, lilacs, variegated box
Are there in plenty, and such hardy flowers
As flourish best untrained. Adjoining these
Are herbs and esculents; and farther still
A field; then cottages with trees, and last
The distant hills and sky.

Bockhampton at this time. A road was to be made at the verge of the wild, uncultivated heathland, giving access to building plots in what would be called New Bockhampton. Only one plot as yet had the name of its intended occupier written in: J. Hardy.

Such was the origin of what has become a literary mecca for visitors from virtually every country where *Tess of the d'Urbervilles* and Hardy's other master-pieces are appreciated. How different it must have been for Hardy's grandparents when they first moved in! For friendly neighbours all they had were the wild ponies that cropped the heath. The place was so lonely that smugglers used the cottage as a temporary store. The lash of a whip at night on the bedroom window was the signal for Mr Hardy to go down and bring in kegs of brandy, carried inland from some point on the Dorset coast between Weymouth Bay and Lulworth Cove.

It may seem an austere and unpromising context to nurture the genius of a poet, but there were elements of a rich tradition in Hardy's parents and grandparents and in the surrounding countryside. When he was 75, Hardy recalled the atmosphere of his birthplace in one of his best-loved poems, 'The Oxen', describing the little group of children sitting by the fire and listening to the stories told by their elders:

Christmas Eve, and twelve of the clock.
  'Now they are all on their knees,'
An elder said as we sat in a flock
  By the embers in hearthside ease.

We pictured the meek mild creatures where
  They dwelt in their strawy pen,
Nor did it occur to one of us there
  To doubt they were kneeling then.

So fair a fancy few would weave
  In these years! Yet, I feel,
If someone said on Christmas Eve,
  'Come; see the oxen kneel

'In the lonely barton by yonder coomb
  Our childhood used to know,'
I should go with him in the gloom,
  Hoping it might be so.

Thomas Webster's painting of 1847, *The Village Choir*, celebrates the fast vanishing world of rural church music recalled in Hardy's *Under the Greenwood Tree*.

The boy's imagination was stimulated by such legends, by folk-tales and memories of the Napoleonic wars, by anecdotes of savage oppression and the contrasting gaiety of rustic music, of dancing and song. Sitting 'by the embers in hearthside ease', Hardy quietly absorbed the raw materials that he later fashioned into his stories.

It was a musical household. The Hardy men played violin or cello in their church until the new taste for organ or harmonium drove village musicians from their galleries. They also played for dances in barns and farmhouses. Hardy's mother had a store of old ballads and folk-songs. Hardy himself was taught to play an instrument as soon as he could hold one, and he was passionately fond of dancing. In old age he would readily demonstrate the ancient style of dancing and pick up a fiddle to recall a traditional tune. If ghostly sounds may linger in the cottage at Bockhampton – Higher Bockhampton as it has become – they would be distant echoes of hymn and carol, of a voice singing 'The Spotted Cow', of feet dancing to the call of 'cross hands and down the middle', or the leaping rhythm of fiddles in 'The Dashing White Sergeant'.

Hardy's father, Thomas the Second, was a convivial man who made his own cider from the apple-trees the grandparents had planted in the cottage orchard. Until he was 33 and soon to be married, Hardy always liked to be at home in the autumn to help his father make the cider – a task, he wrote, 'whose sweet smells and oozings in the crisp autumn air can never be forgotten by those who have had a hand in it'.

In the normal course of events Hardy would have learnt the stone-mason's trade and taken part in the family business – as his younger brother Henry did later – but their mother had higher ambitions for her elder son. An arrangement was made with a Dorchester architect to employ him as a pupil-draughtsman when he left school in July 1856. Here he completed his articled apprenticeship and stayed on until he was nearly 22, when he decided to try his luck in a larger world and took the train to London in April 1862. By good fortune he quickly found employment with a distinguished architect of the period, Sir Arthur Blomfield.

Hardy later liked to claim that he knew 'every street and alley west of St Paul's like a born Londoner, which he was often supposed to be' as a result of the five years he spent there. As a young man, eager to develop his intellectual powers, he took full advantage of what London could offer in its theatres, exhibitions, picture galleries, museums and public meetings. He heard Dickens and John Stuart Mill speak and he came under the spell of Swinburne's latest volume, *Poems and Ballads* (1866).

At night, in his modest digs, he began to see himself as a poet. He was reading extensively and experimenting with verse forms. No editor gave any encouragement to these early efforts, but Hardy's lifelong ambition was now formed. More than anything else he wished to write one poem good enough to be included in some *Golden Treasury* of the future – an ambition that never wavered and ultimately was more than fulfilled. In practical terms, however, there was no prospect of making a living by writing poetry. Realistically, the way ahead was in architecture.

The demands that London made on his health and stamina were such that in the

This view of the 'madding crowd' on Ludgate Hill by Gustave Doré would have been a familiar scene to Hardy in the 1860s, when he was living in London. As a young man he eagerly read Swinburne's poems, 'walking along the crowded London streets, to my imminent risk of being knocked down'.

summer of 1867 Hardy decided to return home and resume employment with the Dorchester architect John Hicks. At the same time his thoughts turned from poetry to the writing of a novel. There was a vast readership for fiction published in serial form; if he aspired to become a professional author, and not simply a versifier in his leisure-time, it must be as a novelist.

His first attempt, *The Poor Man and the Lady*, was never published but it won enough encouragement from Frederick Macmillan and George Meredith to persuade Hardy to persevere. *Desperate Remedies*, a complicated blend of romance and mystery, did achieve publication in 1871, but it was at the third attempt that he really began to find his distinctive style – in *Under the Greenwood Tree* (1872). This drew its inspiration directly from the cottage and the intimate neighbourly world of family elders and village worthies.

Part of the book was written in the cottage, probably at weekends in Hardy's bedroom looking out over the garden and the cider-orchard, and part was written in lodgings at Weymouth, where Hardy's employment had taken him after the death of John Hicks. A Weymouth architect, G.R.Crickmay, had acquired Hicks's practice and invited Hardy to carry on the uncompleted ecclesiastical

(*Far left*) From the bedroom window of Hardy's Cottage can still be seen the cider orchard where Hardy liked to join his father each year in the task of cider-making.

(*Left*) Hardy at about the time he first visited St Juliot.

Weymouth Bay, painted by Constable in the time of Hardy's grandparents when it was a haunt of smugglers. Hardy wrote part of *Under the Greenwood Tree* in Weymouth where he lodged intermittently between 1869 and 1872.

restoration work in which he specialised. By March 1870 only one such project was still awaiting attention – the restoration of a little church on the north coast of Cornwall. At Crickmay's request Hardy made an early start on the cross-country journey which brought him at nightfall to St Juliot rectory. The rector was confined to bed with gout and being attended to by his wife, so it was his wife's sister, Emma Gifford, who received the young architect.

> There was a rumble at the door,
> A draught disturbed the drapery,
> And but a minute passed before,
>   With gaze that bore
>   My destiny,
> The man revealed himself to me.

It was a classic case of love at first sight, or very nearly so. Emma became Hardy's constant companion as he measured and sketched in the dilapidated

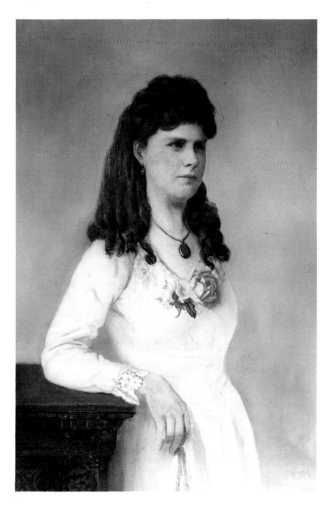

Emma Lavinia Gifford, Hardy's 'West-of-Wessex Girl' and future wife, as she was when they first met at St Juliot in north Cornwall.

Emma Gifford's sketch of the dilapidated St Juliot church in 1870, when Hardy arrived to begin his restoration work.

(*Facing page*) St Juliot: the restored church as it is today. Hardy specialised in ecclesiastical architecture before he turned to a literary career.

church, and – in a holiday mood – explored the surrounding countryside. A particular pleasure was to walk beside the little Valency river as it sparkled and tumbled over rushing falls, among smooth boulders and quiet pools, to reach the sea at Boscastle. When Hardy returned to Dorset, it was, in his words, 'with magic in my eyes'.

That sense of a special magic in the north coast of Cornwall – 'Lyonnesse' as he always named it in legendary Arthurian style – never left him. Boscastle, with its surrounding cliffs and hills, was a place 'of dream and mystery'. When he made his second visit in August 1870, he and Emma took a picnic hamper with their sketching and painting materials and sat beside the Valency under a canopy of oak leaves, where Hardy sketched Emma as she knelt and tried to recover a tumbler that she had dropped when she rinsed it in the stream. Many years later Hardy recalled the incident in one of his finest poems, 'Under the Waterfall'. How many visitors have since tried to guess which of the numerous deep pools might still hide that tumbler!

Inevitably his next novel, *A Pair of Blue Eyes* (1873), had a Cornish setting,

Searching for the glass – (watercolour sketching in Valency valley)

(*Left*) Hardy's sketch of Emma searching for the picnic tumbler she dropped in the Valency river: an episode in their courtship immortalised in his poem 'Under the Waterfall'.

(*Right*) The Valency Valley: in *Some Recollections* Emma recalled that 'often we walked down the beautiful Valley to Boscastle harbour, with a sparkling little brook going the same way'.

Boscastle today, preserved by the National Trust in much the same style as Hardy and Emma knew it in the 1870s.

with Boscastle thinly disguised as 'Castle Boterel', and his walks with Emma to Pentargan Bay and Beeny Cliff woven into the drama of the story. He continued to pay occasional visits to St Juliot, to supervise the restoration of the church and, when that was completed, in a recognised courtship which led to their marriage in September 1874.

It was a time of momentous decision for Hardy. Architecture offered him steady employment at a humdrum level. His three published novels held out the promise of future success but with small rewards as yet and no security. His mother, proud of her son's place in the profession she had chosen for him, must have echoed the sentiments of that fictional mother, Mrs Chickerel, in *The Hand of Ethelberta* (1876): 'A story-teller seems such an impossible castle-in-the-air sort of a trade for getting a living by'. However, there were two new factors to be weighed: *Far from the Madding Crowd* (1874), running as a serial in *The Cornhill*, had established Hardy as a rival to George Eliot; and Emma's romantic temperament supported

'Castle Boterel' – the name Hardy gave to Boscastle in *A Pair of Blue Eyes* (1873). This view of the harbour was the frontispiece to the 1895 edition.

Corfe Castle, which figures prominently in *The Hand of Ethelberta*. This watercolour is by Turner, an artist for whom Hardy had a deep admiration, describing his work as 'a landscape plus a man's soul'. It was given to the National Trust in 1982.

(*Facing page*) Fontmell Down in Dorset. This downland landscape is typical of Hardy's Wessex and was bought for the National Trust by public appeal in 1977.

the idea of marriage to a novelist struggling to win fame. And so his marriage and his dedication to a literary career began simultaneously.

After short spells of 'gipsying' at various addresses in London and Dorset, Hardy bought some furniture to install in a house he had rented at Sturminster Newton. Here he and Emma enjoyed their happiest time together in what he described as a 'two-year idyll'. The immediate surroundings of their house, overlooking the River Stour, inspired several poems, but for the setting of a new novel Hardy's thoughts were drawn back to his birthplace and the great heath of his childhood. In *Under the Greenwood Tree* and *Far from the Madding Crowd* Hardy had concentrated on individual characters, with a subsidiary interest in where they lived. The familiar indoor scenes at Mellstock and Weatherbury are of church and cottage, barn and farmhouse, while out-of-doors it is the needs and procedures of agriculture that shape and dominate the land. In *The Return of the Native* (1878) it is Egdon Heath itself that comes to dominate the lives of those who move across it. With his deepening interest in what he had named as 'Wessex'

Egdon Heath. Probably the most celebrated of Hardy's imaginative landscapes, appearing in verse, short stories and particularly *The Return of the Native*: this is the frontispiece to the 1895 edition.

On the outskirts of Dorchester Max Gate was ready for Hardy and Emma to occupy on 29 June 1885.

Hardy drew on that 'spirit of place' which is now recognised as his hallmark. The brooding heathland contained an elemental force of its own. 'Civilisation', Hardy wrote, 'was its enemy.'

The year 1878 marked a new phase when the Hardys returned to London, perhaps from a feeling that Hardy should now move in the literary circles of the capital. He took advantage of the availability of the British Museum to research the Napoleonic period that provided the story of *The Trumpet-Major* (1880), and he wrote another novel in London, *A Laodicean* (1881), which failed to measure up to what was now expected of him. To make matters worse he had a serious and protracted illness while writing *A Laodicean*, which evidently convinced him that

Then followed the custom-kept rout, shout and flare
Of a skimmity-ride through the naibourhood
('The Bride-Night Fire')

The Wessex custom of 'riding the Skimmington' also features in *The Mayor of Casterbridge*
and is strikingly illustrated in this Jacobean plaster relief at Montacute House in Somerset.
The effigies of violent or unfaithful spouses were paraded through the streets amid general din.

The most personal
elements from Hardy's
study at Max Gate are now
on view in a reconstructed
setting in the County
Museum at Dorchester.

the bewildered disapproval of Emma, whose conventional attitudes were threatened and whose own marriage was drifting into disillusion and estrangement. The intensity of moral argument centred in characters like Tess and Jude won critical acclaim and a wide readership for Hardy, but at a price. Hurt by the attacks on him he decided to give up writing novels at the height of his success, and instead to follow his heart's desire and concentrate on poetry. The publication of *Wessex Poems* in 1898 signalled a new direction in Hardy's work.

Another change at about the same time was his acquisition of a bicycle which gave him the freedom and mobility to explore Wessex more widely and intimately than ever before. He was now able to renew his acquaintance with Glastonbury and Wells, to see 'Sad Sedgemoor' and the hills of Mendip, and to ride into

Dorchester became Hardy's 'Casterbridge', and provided this frontispiece to *The Mayor of Casterbridge*.

Glastonbury Tor in Somerset – a landmark for the trampwoman:

Beneath us figured tor and lea,
From Mendip to the western sea –
I doubt if finer sight there be
Within this royal realm

('A Trampwoman's Tragedy')

(*Facing page*) Hardy acquired his first bicycle in 1895 and found a
new freedom in his explorations of Wessex.

Bristol. Much of the detail in the grand design of his 'partly real, partly dream' country is to be found in his poems, with 'A Trampwoman's Tragedy' as an outstanding example.

The dawning of the present century found Hardy immersed in his most ambitious and innovative work, the verse drama entitled *The Dynasts*. This blended together the dramatic narrative skill of the novelist, the versifying of the poet, and the lifelong interest in the Napoleonic wars that had impelled Hardy to visit the battlefield of Waterloo, to seek out veterans who had fought under Wellington, and to undertake the research embodied in *The Trumpet-Major*. His grandfather had lived through the years when every Dorset man expected the call to resist a French invasion, and Hardy's imagination was fired by such memories. From Max Gate he could see the monument which honours Nelson's captain, that other distinguished bearer in Dorset of the name Hardy, to whom Thomas liked to feel he was related. Here, on Blackdown – as on Rainbarrow and Badbury Rings – the beacon fires had been ready to blaze as signals of an enemy landing. From Portugal to Moscow *The Dynasts* traces its epic drama, but always interleaved with the watchful folk of an embattled Wessex in their familiar settings. At the height of the invasion alarm Keziar Cantle gossips about Napoleon's alleged taste for human flesh: 'Rashers o' baby every morning for breakfast – for all the world like the Cernel Giant in old ancient times!'

The Edwardian decade seemed to set the seal on Hardy's career. *The Dynasts* was completed; two more volumes of collected poems were published; an opera based on *Tess* was performed at Covent Garden, in the presence of Queen Alexandra on the opening night, which he attended; and in 1910 he received the Order of Merit. He was now 70 and might be expected to have little more to add.

The death of his wife in 1912 had the extraordinary effect, however, of releasing a new burst of poetic energy. For years he and Emma had preserved their marriage as a mere shell of respectability, but her death reawakened loving memories of their earlier days and filled him with a sense of remorse. In the following spring he made a pilgrimage to the scenes of their courtship, so timed that he re-entered her 'olden haunts' on the very day they had first met, 43 years before. Once again the majesty of the towering Cornish cliffs and 'the opal and the sapphire of that wandering western sea' stirred the poet's imagination. In his mind's eye he could see 'a ghost-girl-rider' – the young Emma, now a voiceless ghost, who drew him on to revisit, and in his poetry to commemorate, 'the spots we knew when we haunted here together'. In the Valency Valley the lost picnic-tumbler was to be recalled as a

After Emma's death Hardy was drawn back to the towering cliffs of the north Cornwall coast by memories of their early romantic days together.

(*Left*) The Hardy Monument: visible from Max Gate and a reminder of the 'other' Hardy, Nelson's captain, who appears in *The Trumpet-Major* and *The Dynasts*.

(*Right*) The Cerne Abbas Giant: 'They say that Bonaparte lives upon human flesh, and has rashers o' baby every morning for breakfast – for all the world like the Cernel Giant in old ancient times!' (*The Dynasts*)

Tintagel Castle; watercolour by Samuel Palmer, *c*.1848. Chosen by Hardy as the setting for his verse-drama, *The Famous Tragedy of the Queen of Cornwall*.

chalice untouched by human lips since he and Emma 'sipped lovers' wine' from it. At Pentargan Bay he saw

> The waterfall, above which the mist-bow shone
>   At the then fair hour in the then fair weather,
> And the cave just under, with a voice still so hollow
>   That it seems to call out to me from forty years ago,
>   When you were all aglow,
> And not the thin ghost that I now frailly follow!

In the following years he continued to explore in his poems the course of the romance with his 'West-of-Wessex girl' which had begun so strikingly at St Juliot and Boscastle, when 'Our days were a joy, and our paths through flowers'. Nor was Tintagel overlooked. After a second visit in 1916 Hardy began to write his last large-scale work, a verse-drama of Iseult the Fair, Queen of Cornwall, which he completed in 1923. Characteristically he recalled that in Cornwall he had found 'an Yseult of my own'.

His long life ended in 1928. Never did a writer metaphorically sign his name across the English countryside more vividly than Hardy. He might claim that his Wessex was imaginary, a 'partly dream' country, but it touches reality at so many points, great and small. Under his pen the famous landscapes flourish – the heathland of Egdon, the fertile valley of the Froom with its great dairies, the Vale of Blackmoor and the chalk downs that overlook it, Cornwall's haunting 'Lyonnesse' and the western sea. These are the grand set pieces, but so often it is a smaller detail that catches the reader's attention – a manor house, an ancient earthwork, an inn, a headland. So much that is precious to us in the West Country is there for us to enjoy in Hardy's stories and poems, and happily much of it is in the safe and caring hands of the National Trust.

Badbury Rings.